Quick Relief for
Sunday School
Teachers

Group
Loveland, Colorado

Quick Relief for **Sunday School Teachers**

Copyright © 1998 Group Publishing, Inc.

Credits
Contributors: David Arnold, Keith D. Johnson, and Rhonica D. Sheng
Editor: Beth Rowland Wolf
Chief Creative Officer: Joani Schultz
Copy Editor: Pamela Shoup
Art Director and Designer: Kari K. Monson
Cover Art Director: Jeff A. Storm
Cover Designer: SD&F Marketing Communications
Computer Graphic Artist: Eris Klein
Illustrators: Randy Glasbergen, Doug Hall, John McPherson, Rob Portlock, and Ron Wheeler
Production Manager: Peggy Naylor

Library of Congress Cataloging-in-Publication Data
Quick relief for Sunday school teachers.
      p.   cm.
   ISBN 0-7644-2073-9
   1. Christian education--Teaching methods.   2. Sunday school teachers.   I. Group Publishing.
   BV1534.Q53   1998
   268' .6--dc21   98-16015
                                    CIP

10 9 8 7 6 5 4 3 2 1 07 06 05 04 03 02 01 00 99 98
Printed in the United States of America.

Contents

Introduction

Welcome to *Quick Relief for Sunday School Teachers!*

Teaching children in the church is a great privilege, and it's a lot of fun, too. But most church volunteers aren't professional educators. Volunteers come from all walks of life. And often volunteers have a lot of questions about how to best teach the children in their classrooms. This book will offer you lots of practical help that you'll find very worthwhile.

That's because the issues addressed in this book come from children's volunteers just like you. We chose the top issues that Children's Ministry Magazine readers asked about in reader surveys and asked professional children's ministers to offer the advice that they'd give to teachers in their churches.

In this book, you'll find helpful answers to your questions about teaching, kids' educational needs, how to teach the Bible, and how to cultivate quality relationships with the children you see each week. Through the answers in this book, you'll feel prepared for ministry, you'll be encouraged, and you'll find enthusiasm for working with children.

We hope that the answers you find in this book will help you fully enjoy your work with children. Teaching children to love God is a blessing full of joy. Happy reading!

Quick Relief for
Teachers

I said I'd teach, but I don't know how. Where do I start?

So you have agreed to teach the children in your church and now realize that saying "yes" was the easy part. Whether this creates a mini-crisis or exuberant enthusiasm, the first order of business should be to pray for your students and for yourself. God has given you a willing heart and can give you the ability to teach your students.

● **Remember the goal.** Remember that your prime objective is to teach children about Jesus and to help them grow in their understanding of who God is and what God has done. Don't allow yourself to be overwhelmed with the responsibility for kids' entire spiritual future—that's God's responsibility. You are there to be a guide and teach God's Word in a memorable, meaningful way.

● **Think like a child.** Once you've had a chance to pray about your new teaching responsibility, think back to when you were the age of the children in your class. Try to remember how you felt, what was important to you, what was fun or not fun, and how you learned best. Think about teachers who made learning fun. Make a list of activities or hobbies you enjoyed then and now. Your list might include music, drama, storytelling, reading, art, painting, clay or modeling dough, games, creative writing, and science. Then consider how to incorporate some of these activities into your curriculum. For example, if you're teaching a lesson on Noah's ark, you might have the students read a poem about animals, make a boat from craft sticks, or each write a story as if they were there with Noah.

● **Be comfortable in the classroom.** Students will have more fun and learn more when their teacher feels comfortable and at ease. Plan your lesson early, and be fully prepared when class time arrives. Teaching a sixty- to ninety-minute class is a privilege—respect the trust you've been given by spending plenty of time preparing. Here's a workable preparation schedule that will help you make the most of your time with children:

Day 1: Reflect on your last lesson. Think about what went well and what didn't; what worked and what didn't. Consider things that you might change or keep the same. Call any students who were absent, and invite them back next week. Send postcards to any students who were ill. Mail birthday cards to those who have birthdays this week.

Day 2: Read through the next lesson, and begin to envision how this lesson will work for your class. Pray for guidance.

Day 3: Pray for God to lead you in preparation. Read through your lesson again. Make a list of what you'll need.

Day 4: Pray for your students. Make final preparations in planning your lesson. Prepare any samples of crafts or work sheets. Take care of all final details. Check in with co-teachers if you have not already done so.

Day 5: Take a break. Allow God to let the lesson sink into your own heart. Pray for the children, your co-teachers, and the children's ministry leaders.

Day 6: Read through the lesson again. Have you missed anything? Do you need to change anything? Commit your plans to the Lord. Pray that you will handle God's Word correctly and have a good understanding of your students and their needs. If you have access to the building Friday or Saturday, you may want to take everything to your classroom and have it available for a substitute teacher in the event you are unexpectedly delayed or unable to teach. (You may want to have a different lesson plan with supplies made up ahead of time and stored in your classroom for a substitute teacher.)

Day 7: Have fun, and be flexible. Arrive at least fifteen to twenty minutes early to get ready, and have everything laid out for the class. Greet children at the door, and welcome them with a smile. Your room should be open, bright, colorful, inviting, warm, pleasant, and fun. Although some of that depends

For some reason, Daniel began to feel uneasy.

9

on the lighting, bulletin boards, and posters, most of it depends on your attitude. If you are rushed, overwhelmed, and frustrated, children will feel that as well.

How do I keep my enthusiasm?

When people work hard, even at tasks they love, it's easy to get worn out and lose enthusiasm. But there are many things we can do to stay enthusiastic about teaching children. Here are some ideas:

● *Stay connected to God.* Keep your relationship with God fresh and vital by praying consistently and reading Scripture. Treat God as you would your best friend. Be intentional about making time to spend with God. You'll find that God gives you enthusiasm for the tasks he wants you to do.

● *Cultivate joy, love, and obedience to God.* Read John 15:9-17 and note how joy, love, and obedience are connected. Joy comes when we love and obey God. And joy is a key to enthusiasm.

● *Stay connected with other Christians.* Make friends with other Christians, and spend time with them, perhaps in Bible study and mutual encouragement or just having fun. Be sure you make time for Christian relationships.

● *Stay connected to children.* As teachers, our best motivation comes from our love for children. Get to know the children in your class. Know their needs, their fears, and their joys. Listen to them, and enjoy their company. Pray for them regularly. When you're connected to kids, you'll be excited to teach them about God.

● *Vary your routine.* People get bored when they do the same thing over and over. Increase your enthusiasm (and your students' enthusiasm) by doing something new and different. Meet outside. Have a party. Play games at the beginning instead of the end. Put the work sheets away, and put on a Bible story play or hold a Bible quiz show. No matter what your routine is, everyone will get a lift from a change.

Remember that changing your routine means you have to be organized and plan in advance. One "enthusiasm-squelcher" is not allowing enough time to plan for an interesting lesson. If

you generally look at the lesson the night before or on the way to church, you can bet that your enthusiasm for teaching won't last long. Start planning several days in advance of the lesson, and you'll find your anticipation will grow.

● **Recharge your batteries.** One great way to gain enthusiasm is to meet with other children's workers to share ideas. Talk with the ministry coordinator in your church, and arrange to go to a local convention. There are children's ministry fellowships that meet in many areas. Another place to look for new ideas is at your local Christian book store. You'll find many resources on children's ministry that are guaranteed to boost your enthusiasm.

My kids love music, but I'm not musical. What do I do?

The idea of using music in the classroom is often enough to fill nonmusical teachers with nail-biting anxiety. But there are lots of easy ways to include music in your class without being a virtuoso.

● **Use a tape or CD.** Most curricula come with a tape or CD that you can use in your classroom. Beyond that, there is an amazing array of good music choices at almost any Christian book store.

Find a reliable tape recorder (or CD player), and make sure it has a counter so you can cue up a song that the kids can sing along with. Don't assume that you have to manage the recorder either. Have one of the students be the "music manager" who cues the tape and presses "play" on your instruction.

● **Involve children in leading songs.** After kids learn a song, have them lead the music. If students are younger, pick a special "music leader," and have him or her stand next to you to lead the children.

● **Recruit a music team or individual.** Many people love to sing but they can't teach. Combine their skill with your need, and make a great classroom team!

● **Use videos.** There are many music videotapes available, too. Cue up the song before class, and let the video lead the children in singing.

● **Remember that music in the classroom doesn't require**

singing. Many children enjoy simply listening to music. You can have children listen to instrumental or vocal tapes, CD's, and videos.

How can I get my spouse to understand my passion for this "extra" volunteer activity?

The support of a spouse makes all the difference in our motivation, focus, and creativity. To not have his or her support is unfortunate, but it isn't the end of the world. A spouse's opposition, however, can make you miserable, and it can negatively affect your teaching. Here are some things you can do to help your spouse learn to understand and support your ministry:

● **Pray.** Ask God to help your spouse give the encouragement and support you need.

● **Let your spouse see what you do.** Invite your spouse to watch you teach. Explain your plans. Share your dreams. Talk about the children and how much they mean to you.

● **Be responsible with how you use your time.** Make sure that your ministry doesn't steal from your family time. No matter how passionate you are about ministry, you still have responsibilities to your own family. If things at home are neglected or if your relationship with your spouse suffers because of your commitment to ministry, your spouse may be resentful. Are you connecting with your family daily?

● **Explore opportunities for your spouse to get involved.** Maybe your service merely deepens insecurity in your spouse because he or she is not serving. Consider team teaching or letting your spouse lead crafts or singing.

What do I need to know about safety?

We must provide a safe and secure environment for children. Although accidents will occur even in the safest environments, we can take measures to protect ourselves and our churches from child abuse, carelessness, or a dangerous environment. Here are some things to be aware of:

● **A safe space.** Inspect your classroom, your church, your parking lot, and your neighborhood to help ensure that kids are safe. If you work with babies, providing a safe classroom means disinfecting all surfaces, washing your hands after diaper changes, putting childproof locks on cabinets, and putting protective covers on electrical outlets. If you work with older children, providing a safe space might mean that you play active games in the fellowship hall instead of in a small, furniture-packed classroom. Keeping older children safe may also mean that you need to supervise and protect children who walk home after an event.

● *Safe supervision.* It's very important that there always be at least two adults supervising children. This way, if a child gets hurt and needs attention, one adult can assist the child and the other adult can supervise the rest of the children. This team protects children from potential abuse situations, and it protects adults from false accusations of abuse.

Some children's workers get caught up in the activities and become participants instead of supervisors. It's great to join in the lesson and the fun of your class time, but it's also important to remember that you're responsible for the safety of the children in your class. Don't get so involved that you forget to be watchful.

We don't have enough time to teach. What do we do?

Lots of people have this problem. Sometimes the issue is that there's too much material to cover. Sometimes the issue is that children straggle into class and you waste a good portion of class time waiting for everyone to arrive. In some cases, the problem may really be that there isn't enough time scheduled to teach. The first thing to do is to figure out why you don't have enough time to teach. Then you can address the real problem.

● *Too much material.* If you have too many activities to squeeze into your teaching time, carefully study the lesson each week, and pick the activities you'd most like children to do. This way you won't feel rushed. There's no reason to feel that you have to get through the entire lesson each week. By picking out a few activities, you can choose the strongest part of the lesson. This way your time with kids will be used to its best advantage.

● **Waiting for kids to arrive.** One way to combat this problem is to make your class so interesting the kids want to get there early. You might want to provide scrumptious treats for only the first ten minutes of class. You might want to schedule games first or some other kind of fun project. Kids will be excited to arrive early and enjoy the fun you've planned.

Another way to combat this problem is to simply accept that you'll have a shorter class time because of lateness. Cut back the number of activities you plan for the class time, and make the time you do have as captivating as possible. You may find that when kids really enjoy a class, they make an effort to get there earlier.

If kids are late because their parents can't find a parking place or because the church service regularly runs late, talk with your pastor about ways to solve these problems.

● **Too little time on the schedule.** If your class time is scheduled to last for less than forty-five minutes, talk with your pastor or your church board about lengthening the allotted time. With a forty-five-minute teaching time, kids will be in Christian education less than forty hours a year.

Considering the importance of Christian education, you need to do everything you can to maximize your time with kids. Cut out activities that seem like busywork. Focus on activities that will result in real learning.

Our ministry is great, but kids aren't regular in their attendance. What can I do to promote regular attendance?

● **Strongly communicate how much children are missed when they are not there.** Send postcards, e-mail (really!), missed lessons, or a note to the children. Your extra attention will let kids know they're a special part of the class.

● **Look into why they are missing so often.** Problems could be in their control, your control, or someone else's control.

Many kids can choose whether or not to go to church with their parents, or they may be spending the night with a friend. You can control the lesson content to ensure that it's meaningful and interesting for kids. Unfortunately you can't control a custodial issue (two weeks with one parent and two weeks with another) or if a family is on vacation.

● *Invite kids for special occasions.* Mail a notice telling them about something happening next week that is extra special. Don't shame them for not attending, but give them a reason to come back.

● *Avoid attendance charts.* Charts simply alienate kids by displaying their "failures." Instead encourage attendance in a positive way through random parties, treats, games, videos, or other fun surprises.

How do I best use my time with kids?

Don't waste children's time. You waste time by lecturing, making kids sit still, and allowing disruptions to rule the room. You put time to its best use when you...

● *Focus on a goal for the lesson time.* Make it simple, make it achievable, and make it memorable. Having a focus gives you a measure of whether you are using time wisely and effectively.

● *Challenge kids with material that is stimulating and effective.* Pay attention to their interest level and to their abilities. Don't plan too many thinking activities if your kids are kinesthetic learners. Don't plan reading activities if your kids aren't confident readers. It your kids are captivated by a puppet play, by all means introduce puppets in class.

● *Over plan for class.* Plan for more than you can do in the hour, but prioritize the activities so you know which activities you most want to cover. If an activity works well, be ready to spend more time on it. If an activity bombs, have another activity ready to put in its place.

● *Are enthusiastic.* Be crazy about kids. And be wild for the Bible. The kids will catch your enthusiasm!

Is competition really all that bad?

There are many negatives to competition. Use these guidelines to help understand how competition can cause division and hard feelings between children:

● *In general, it's best to avoid competition whenever possible.* Competition can leave children with the impression that a teacher's love or God's love is based on works, Bible memory, perfect attendance, or whatever spiritual goal has been placed before them. We want children to see church as a place of unconditional love and complete acceptance. That's hard to do when kids are pitted against each other in competitive activities. Uncontrolled, competition can destroy a classroom that is otherwise based on encouragement and positive reinforcement. It can also cultivate pride and jealousy.

● *There are ways to put a positive spin on competition.* Instead of having children compete against each other, have them compete against themselves or against the clock. Children can encourage one another while they seek to beat their own records. While we want a child's church experience to be one of love and acceptance, it's an indisputable fact that children will encounter competition throughout their lives. We can seek to minimize the competitiveness kids experience at church, but we should also seek to teach children how to deal with competition as a Christian. Mildly competitive experiences can be great ways for us to teach children how to be good sports, how to encourage and support a rival, and how to always do their best.

Before you decide to put competition into place in your classroom, think seriously and clearly about what you are trying to accomplish by having the children compete. Unless you're specifically trying to teach them to deal with competition positively, it's probably best to avoid competitive activities.

Only one kid showed up for my program. What should I have done?

Yikes! It's easy to take it personally when we plan an event and the children don't come. But chances are the low attendance has more to do with planning than anything else. Use these ideas to boost attendance at special events:

● *Make sure it's an event children want to come to.* Ask the children what they like to do before you begin to plan. Even if you're planning a service project, you can almost always tailor the activity to the interests of the children in your class.

● *Check everybody's schedule.* If you schedule a big event on the same day as the school carnival, you may be disappointed in the turnout for your event. Check the church calendar as well as local school calendars. Also check out the city recreation calendar if you have a lot of children involved in city sports leagues.

● *Don't plan too much.* Families get overwhelmed with events if they have more than one child. Be sensitive to how often you plan events and how expensive you make them. Five dollars may seem cheap for an entire afternoon's activities. But for a family with four children, it's a big expense.

● *Promote the event well.* This includes planning enough time for everyone to put it on the calendar and look forward to it. If you spring an event on kids and families, their calendars may already be full. Also, kids should have enough time to really anticipate an event. If you plan too far in advance, kids will get weary of waiting and will move on to something else. Start to promote your event four to six weeks before the event.

Also, don't count on kids to get the message home. Mail postcards, put up posters in the church, and mention the event to parents you see before and after class time.

● *Make the best of it no matter how many kids come.* Even if only two children come, you can have a great time. Maybe your plans for a pizza party or a summer Olympics won't be possible, but you and those two children can go out for ice cream. What an opportunity to make friends with the children in your group!

How do I teach a very small or a very large class?

There are challenges and rewards in teaching both very small classes and very large classes. Try some of these ideas:

● *Small classes.* You'll find the most success in teaching a small class when you make the most of its size rather than wishing you had just a few more kids to fill up the room.

Having a very small class is an incredible opportunity to invest in the lives of individuals. While there are some things that are simply impossible to pull off with a small class—such as playing large-group games or putting on big dramas—the benefits far outweigh the disadvantages.

With a small class, you can truly get to know every child you teach. Then you can guide and encourage children according to their individual needs. As you're teaching a small class, begin to think of the class as more of a discipleship opportunity. Think of yourself as a friend and mentor rather than as a teacher.

You may need to adapt your curriculum to fit the unique needs of a small group. Cut out activities that require more kids than you have. Add activities that kids can do on their own or with a partner. Instead of standing at the front of the class lecturing to two or three students, become a facilitator who guides individual children in an independent study course.

With a small class, it's easier to meet anywhere and any time for Bible study. It's easier to plan events because there are fewer people to contact. You can easily pick up and move your class to the park, to the pancake restaurant, or to the ice-cream parlor. Make the most of this time to make friends and influence a small group of children for Christ.

● **Large classes.** Large classes require that you become a master planner just because of the incredible logistics involved in organizing a large group of wiggly, energetic children. With large classes you have an amazing array of opportunities. A large class can put on a musical, fill up a pizza parlor, or pull off a large service project.

"TO KEEP THE KIDS FROM GETTING OUT? ARE YOU KIDDING?! WE LOCK IT UP TO KEEP THE TEACHERS' FROM GETTING OUT!"

With a large class, you may find that the best strategies involve finding capable assistants to help you guide the children into activities. One technique that works well in large classes is to break the class into smaller groups of five to seven children. Assign a teenage or adult helper to each smaller group, and have the smaller groups rotate through activities that you coordinate. Another technique that works well is to do activities in one large group, and then form smaller groups for discussion. You may find that smaller groups also work well for completing projects and crafts.

One of the challenges with large groups is to make sure that everyone feels connected and involved. If you have more than ten or fifteen kids in a class, it's impossible for you to develop a close relationship with each of them. Find people in your church who'd be willing to be mentors or friends to the kids in your class. Often, teenagers are great in this role.

One of the benefits of large groups is that you can offer a wider variety of activities that are tailored to children's interests. Take advantage of this opportunity by planning many different kinds of events for the children to take part in.

How do I find new, creative ideas week after week?

All teachers suffer from idea burnout. That's when every activity you look at seems old and tired, and you just can't get excited about teaching. Here are some places to look for new ideas:

- Attend the training meetings your church holds.
- Subscribe to a magazine such as Children's Ministry Magazine.
- Get involved with a children's ministry fellowship.
- Make friends with the other teachers in your church and swap ideas.
- Ask your children's ministry pastor about resources you can use.
- Attend a local or regional ministries conference.

- Check out the Internet. Many children's magazines and educational groups have Web sites with tons of fun ideas.
- Contact curriculum publishers and ask about resources. You can also request that they send you catalogs that list their new resources.
- Visit the teacher resources store in your area.
- Spend time in the children's section of your public library. Read the magazines, and peruse craft and game books.
- Make friends with a schoolteacher, and find out what's hot in education.

Quick Relief for
Teaching Kids

Our curriculum is nondenominational. How do I teach about our denominational traditions?

Many churches choose to use nondenominational curriculum. Sometimes that curriculum doesn't include everything you want your children to learn, such as the traditions, doctrinal distinctives, and history of your denomination. Here are some ways to find material to supplement your curriculum:

● **Check with your children's ministry coordinator and your pastor.** Your children's ministry coordinator is likely to have a better idea of the big picture of children's ministry at your church. You may find that your coordinator or pastor has planned to incorporate these things into another aspect of the children's program such as a midweek program or children's church. Or it could be that your coordinator or pastor will want to spend time researching the best way to teach children about your denomination's traditions. Look to your leaders for guidance on this issue.

● **Contact your publisher.** Most curriculum publishers intentionally focus exclusively on key Bible stories and age-appropriate applications because teaching the Bible is their primary objective. Because of their broad market, publishers usually can't address the theological points and practices that are specific to each denomination. However, many publishers redesign their regular curriculum for individual denominations. Contact your publisher to find out if they've modified their curriculum for your denomination.

● **Contact your denominational office.** Some denominations offer their own curriculum for their churches. These materials will teach your denomination's key traditions. You can use this curriculum as a supplement to what you're already using. Be sure to talk with the children's ministry coordinator before you change the curriculum you use.

● **Check with other churches in your denomination.** Other churches in your denomination may have already found supplemental material that will provide the instruction you need. They would probably be happy to share this information with you.

● **Check your local Christian bookstore.** Your local Christian bookstore is one of the best places to find the latest and best materials available to churches today. Explain your need to the

Christian education consultant and see what he or she suggests. The bookstore staff usually knows what other churches are doing and what curriculum is effective for your geographic and demographic area.

● **Write your own supplementary curriculum.** This is a little more involved, but could be well worth your time. First, list all the traditions you desire to introduce or explain to your students. Next, research bookstores and libraries for the information you desire to teach. Finally, write the lessons using age-appropriate teaching methods. You may surprise yourself at how well these original lessons come out and how much your class will appreciate your hard work. You may want to get parents involved in helping you with this project. Make sure you have your pastor check out your work before you begin teaching.

Some kids in my church are home-schooled, and they know a lot about the Bible. How do I maintain their interest?

More and more children attend school at home. Many of them use high quality, Christian-based curricula which help students begin building a foundation of Bible knowledge sooner than their public school peers. Students may spend a greater amount of time learning key Bible stories and may have more time to explore the applications of those stories to their lives. Home-schoolers with a broad biblical foundation can be a real asset in your class.

Here are a some suggestions for helping home-schooled kids blossom in your program:

● **Have home-schoolers each prepare a special report to give during class next week.** This works well when you know what topics they've studied in depth at home.

● **Have home-schooled students lead a small discussion group or activity.** This works well with older children who've studied specific subjects at home. Use this technique infrequently so that home-schoolers aren't set apart from the rest of the class.

● **Deepen their understanding of the Bible.** Often, home-schooled kids know a lot of facts from the Bible. But you can deepen their understanding of Scripture by using various methods. Help these kids increase their understanding of the Bible by building on what they already know. Use questions like these to deepen your discussion of Scripture:

- What does the Bible say? What are the facts ?
- Why does the Bible say it? What is the background?
- What does this fact or story mean to me today?
- What does this tell us about God?
- What does this tell us about the world?
- What does this tell about me? What do I need to change? What do I need to continue doing?

Often students will tell you that they already know the Bible story you're teaching. Students with this attitude will tune you out before you even begin the lesson. However, you can respond to them by saying, "I know you learned this at a younger age, but now let's add to what you know! All your life you will be learning more information about the Bible."

The kids in my class have different backgrounds and abilities. How do I teach so many different kids?

As our society becomes more diverse racially, economically, and politically, churches reflect this changing culture. If there is diversity in your class, you have a class with great potential for learning many important lessons. Here are three keys to effective teaching in a class of students with many backgrounds and abilities:

- **Identify and understand the areas of diversity.** Consider the kids in your class. How are they alike? How are they different? We are blessed when we worship and serve with a diverse mix of people in our churches. The Bible tells us in I Corinthians 12:14-27 that the church is like a body made up of many parts. In this illustration of a body, similarity is actually a weakness, but diversity is needed for strength and effectiveness.

Understanding and appreciating diversity in a class is a key step toward being an effective teacher.

- **Love all the children unconditionally.** John 3:16 tells us that

God loves the whole world. That means God loves everyone, everywhere, for all time. God loves every child in your class no matter his or her shape, size, skin color, economic background, or home situation.

Do you love your children with an individual, unconditional, and limitless love? You'll find that the more you love the individuals in your class, the more they'll accept and love each other. You'll also find that when students feel welcomed and appreciated, they learn more.

● *Strive to reach children and connect them with the group.* The methods used in your classroom will be partly determined by the children you teach. Effective teachers know that one style of teaching can't reach every student. Consider the needs, personalities, and backgrounds of the children you teach. Then vary the activities you use in class based on your individual students.

For example, children learn differently. Some students need action to learn. Other students learn best when they talk or work with their hands. Consider the kinds of activities and projects that your kids get excited about. Those are the kinds of activities that'll make them excited about God. Use as many of those activities as you can.

Also consider your students' backgrounds. Some students may feel out of place in your church because of their skin color or because of their economic situation or even because of what school they go to. Strive to create an atmosphere of community in your classroom. This means developing friendships with your students and encouraging students to develop friendships with each other. Intentionally take time out from the curriculum to allow kids time to get to know each other. Throw parties and go on field trips to give kids time to deepen their friendships. When children have made genuine friendships, many of the problems associated with their diversity will be solved.

How do I get kids to sit still and listen?

It doesn't work to measure how well kids listen by how well they sit still.

● *God made children to wiggle, make noise, and have fun!* Children differ from adults in how they show that they're **25** paying attention to a lesson. As adults, we sit still and focus our quiet attention on the teacher. But children who are engaged in the lesson move as they busily experiment, explore, and learn. Children who are focused on the lesson make noise—a good kind of noise that shows their enthusiasm for the lesson. Children who are interested in the lesson have fun—often they show how much they're learning by how much they laugh.

● **Help children learn when to wiggle, where to make noise, and how to have fun.** Too often, teachers who have trouble getting kids focused on the lesson will try to introduce too many sit-still-and-concentrate activities. They reason that if the kids are bouncing off the walls, adding quiet, focused activities will keep the kids from becoming completely uncontrollable. However, many times kids actually need more activity to help them concentrate and settle down.

Experiment with the kids in your class by offering both quiet activities and active activities. This will help you understand whether your class responds well to quiet activities or whether you really should add more active activities.

● *Tune in to kids' actions.* Sometimes, no matter what kind of activities you offer, the kids will be too wound up to focus on the lesson. When a child can't or won't sit still or become involved in an activity, he or she is communicating a message. Several factors could cause restlessness:

● The child may have a *physical need.* Are kids hungry, tired, or do they need to go to the bathroom?

● The child may have an *emotional need.* Things may not have gone well at home, or there may be some conflict between students in the class.

● The child may have a *spiritual need.* Being in church may be uncomfortable for unchurched kids. The message of the lesson could make them feel guilty, unworthy, or maybe even angry.

● The child may have a *social need.* Becoming restless and encouraging others to be off task could be a result of a child not having enough self-discipline.

Take time to talk to a restless child. Gently probe to discover why he or she can't concentrate, then work together to fix the problem.

How can I tell if kids really are paying attention?

Picture yourself in front of your classroom. You look at the class full of bright-faced children...who are mentally everywhere else on this planet except with you! You attempt to get their attention, but few even know you're in the room. You continue teaching, and the thought keeps crossing your mind, "Is anyone really listening?"

How can you tell if kids really are paying attention? Here are some suggestions to gauge the retention level of your students:

● **Look into children's eyes as you teach.** How often do kids' eyes meet yours? Eye contact indicates that they are listening. When there is little or infrequent eye contact, a child may have something else on his or her mind. This child may be in class today under protest. Or the child may have had a tough morning at home. Sometimes interpersonal relationship problems or loneliness in a class may cause a child to be disconnected from you during the lesson. It will take some time and patience to help get the disconnected student back on track, but it will be worth the effort for both of you. Everyone has bad days, and sometimes these bad times happen before church!

● **Ask questions that require more than a yes or no answer.** It seems as if there are four basic answers to most questions in a child's Christian education class: "yes," "no," "Jesus," and "God." Teachers need to learn to ask good questions. Begin questions with words like "why," "how," and "what if." These produce good, thought-provoking questions that require kids to think. This helps the kids discover the truth for themselves and become excited about what they're learning. When kids have to listen carefully to your questions and think about their answers, they'll be more likely to listen to what you're saying.

● **Listen to the type of noise your class is making.** Not all noise is bad. Some noise may come from children who are right on target with the lesson. Students involved in discussion groups, pair-shares, debates, informal discussions, discovery games, role-plays, and creating projects usually generate a level of noise that is music to a teacher's ears. Children who are always quiet may actually indicate they are lost or have been left behind in the learning process.

How Can I get kids to really experience God rather than just be entertained?

Today, children demand and expect to be entertained. To give them entertainment only is to shortchange them. Besides, there is nothing more interesting, fun, or fulfilling than to grow closer to God and explore his Word. Helping children feel God's love, see God's power, and experience God's grace are the greatest lessons we can teach. There are many very entertaining teaching methods we can use to help a child experience God in a dynamic and life-changing way!

● *Expose kids to as many Bible characters as possible.* God moved in many great and mighty ways as recorded in the Bible. These stories are action-packed and exciting. As your students learn about the lives of historical people from the Bible, they will discover how God can work in their lives. You can help children make the connection that God is just as interested in their lives as he was in the lives of people in the Bible.

● *Use a variety of methods to help children experience God in Sunday school class:*

Prayer—Children develop a relationship with God when they spend time in prayer. Keep track of children's requests and God's answers. This helps children understand God's character and see God's work in their lives.

Music—Children develop a love for God when they sing praises to him. Music also reinforces Bible stories and Christian principles. Music is a great way to have fun while learning about and experiencing God.

Nature studies—Children see God's power when they study creation. Creation shows God's creativity, his love of beauty, and his amazing sense of order. Learning about creation tells children a lot about the Creator.

Role-play—Children can experience God's love, compassion, and forgiveness through drama and role-plays. Children love to play the parts of Bible characters. Experiencing the Bible through drama is a great way to make God feel more real to kids.

Children need more than fun—give them the joy that comes from knowing and following God. Joy brings a greater amount of contentment and fulfillment to life than just having fun. Let's help our children go beyond having fun to the deep satisfying joy of serving God.

How can I get kids to remember their verses for more than one week?

emory is a strange phenomenon. When we stop using what we've committed to memory, we forget it. The same is true with memorizing the Bible. If we don't apply it to our everyday living, we tend to forget it.

Here are some techniques for keeping memory verses fresh in children's minds:

● **Emphasize application.** You'll find that children remember verses better when they do more than just memorize the words. Get the children involved in exploring the meaning of the verse. Explain and illustrate how the verse impacts our everyday living. Brainstorm ways to use the context or concept of the verse in life today or during the coming week. *Making Scripture Memory Fun* (Group Publishing) is a good resource for helping children memorize verses by exploring the meaning of Scripture.

● **Review.** Nothing beats review. People need to revisit material several times before it's committed to long-term memory. Use games, puzzles, activities, and projects to review previous verses. Repeat the same activities that you used to teach the verse, but add small twists to make the activity new. You can also challenge kids to use critical-thinking skills to recall verses they've memorized. For example, ask questions that help children apply Scripture to the circumstances of Bible characters. You might ask, "What Bible verse would you offer to Jonah to help him learn how to respond to God's command that he go to Nineveh?" or "What Bible verse would you use to encourage Paul and Silas when they were in jail?"

● **Keep verses visible in the classroom.** Use posters, banners, pictures, and models as catalysts to help students remember verses from one week to the next. Students can make their own memory helps or use the memory verse items included with the curriculum for each lesson. This step is important because many children only attend class every other week. The visual reinforcement will help them keep up with the class.

- **Have children teach the verses to other students.** Use cards, white boards/chalkboards, wall charts, or puzzles. Teaching their peers actually increases kids' own level of retention.
- **Live out the verse during the week.** Review the verse from the past week, then ask students to share how they used the principle from the verse during the week.

How do I teach the essential Bible facts without boring children?

This is the video game generation. Kids today are much different from the "MTV Generation" or "Generation X." This is the *"Next Generation"*—they are "Generation Y" or the "New Millennial Kids." Typically these children were born after 1983. Much like the video games they play, these kids are always on the move, ready for a change of direction and a greater level of excitement. Life has many options and opportunities. The family car puts on many miles a week getting this generation to the next activity. Any pause in the action of a breakneck schedule puts the Generation Y child in a situation he or she quickly labels as "boring."

How do we teach these children the essential facts of the Bible?

- **Teach the Bible dramatically.** Teach your children the essentials of the Bible in the manner they were written. The Bible is full of drama, complete with villains and heroes, love and jealously, bravery and cowardice. The Bible becomes boring when we teach it as just another book or historical account. The Bible is the living Word of God, sharper than a two-edged sword, containing all we need to know to discover God's love and mercy.
- **Teach with intensity.** The essentials of the Bible—when properly taught—will challenge children and move them to live exciting, Christlike lives. This kind of teaching will not put them to sleep. Getting children excited about God's Word requires us to be excited first. The Bible gives life meaning, direction, and support. It introduces us to the one and only, great, mighty, and wonderful God of the universe! The Bible is

awesome because God is awesome. No teacher who brings kids to a regular, personal encounter with this great book and with this great God will ever be called boring!! Keep the Bible alive in your lessons.

● **Be transparent as you teach.** The Bible is very honest about the lives described in its pages. Scripture tells us about David's failings as well as his successes and Solomon's depression and cynicism as well as his wisdom. We need to be just as honest. You are a living example of someone who has a daily relationship with the one true God. Your actions and words demonstrate for our children how the Bible is currently working in your life. Your firsthand account of how God is working in your life will rarely be called boring.

● **Invite children to meet Jesus.** A wise teacher will also understand that some children in class are bored with the Bible because they don't really know God. The Bible tells us our eyes are closed to the things of God until we know him. Do everything you can to introduce children to God. Encourage them to deepen their relationship with God through prayer and praise. Explain how God worked through the lives of people in the Bible to draw us all closer to him. When children understand God's purpose and God's love, when they see God working in the Bible, then they'll become interested in Scripture.

How do I deal with tough subjects such as creationism vs. evolutionism?

God loves to address tough questions. In fact, the toughest questions children ask are answered in the Bible. Biblical answers to tough questions reveal the infinite depth, width, and height of God's wisdom and knowledge. Here are some suggestions to help you deal with your students' tough questions:

● **Be systematic in your teaching.** By taking a chronological or systematic approach to the Scriptures, most of today's controversial issues will come up in the course of study. Let the Bible raise the topic in an honest, straightforward manner. Then show children what God says and compare it to what others believe. Most curricula cover most of the Bible over the course of several years and therefore cover many issues.

- **Give an answer for the tough questions.** When tough questions come up, take time to discuss them and help children answer them. Whenever appropriate, refer children back to the Bible for the answer. If you don't know the answer to a child's question, don't feel bad. Kids can ask amazingly tough questions. Tell the child that you don't know the answer, but you'll work with the child to find the answer.

- **Keep answers age-appropriate.** Tough issues like creation vs. evolution come up even with very young children. But deep, detailed answers aren't necessary until children are old enough to really understand them. It is often enough to reassure young children that God has an answer to their questions. Focus on answering the question asked rather than giving detailed information that may be confusing. However, be sensitive to kids who are struggling with a tough question. If a child is puzzled by your answer or still seems troubled after you've given a simple explanation, don't be afraid to delve deeper.

- **Make time to talk about difficult questions.** Many tough questions are asked at less than opportune times during a class. You can acknowledge the importance of a child's tough question yet stay on the current subject of the lesson. You can do this by allowing a special time at the end of class to handle tough questions. When a tough question comes up, a teacher can defer it to the "Tough Question Time" because good questions deserve special attention.

Sometimes, though, the tough question may be directly related to your lesson. Take time to answer these questions as they come up—even if it means you don't have time to get to all the activities in your lesson.

I can't get kids to respond to my questions. How do I get them involved?

There are a number of reasons why some children don't like to respond to questions or speak in a classroom setting. Some of those reasons are based on fears children have, so it is important not to force children to speak. Instead, you want to encourage children to share and provide an atmosphere that makes them comfortable and eager to respond to your questions. Here are a few ideas to help:

● **Ask open-ended questions.** Instead of asking, "Where was Jesus born?" ask, "What do you think Bethlehem was like on the night Jesus was born?" Rather than asking children for one correct answer, ask the children to come up with ten different ways to answer your question. Go around the room and let each child tell his or her favorite part of the story from the day's lesson.

● **Let kids talk about themselves.** Begin your class time by sitting in a circle and asking each child to share something that happened to him or her this week. This is an exercise to help children feel more comfortable answering questions in front of the other students.

● **Affirm every child who responds, even if the answer is wrong.** You don't need to agree with every answer, but you can affirm the children by acknowledging their efforts, thanking them for their responses, smiling at them, or by saying, "That's an interesting way to look at it."

● **Let everyone have a turn.** Hand each child a couple of tokens or tickets to spend during the question and answer portion of your lesson. Each time a child answers, he or she should turn in a ticket. This will not only encourage more bashful children to answer, but will help those who have answered every question to understand when it's their turn to listen.

You can also use the phrase, "Let's hear from someone who hasn't answered a question yet today." The child or children who always answer can then take time to listen to other students. If no one volunteers, go ahead and call students by name to answer.

WHAT'S THIS RUMOR I HEAR ABOUT SOME OF YOU
SKIPPING MY SUNDAY SCHOOL CLASS?"

● *Consider how many students are in your class.* Small groups will provide a safer setting for children to speak up. If you have a classroom of thirty children, you'll need some additional helpers to facilitate five or six small groups for discussion time. You can assign each group to come up with its own answer and have one child report from each small group. Responding for the group may not be as scary as coming up with your own answer. If you are the only teacher in a larger class, then you can meet individually with each of the small groups and have a discussion time as part of your class period.

The most important thing you can do to help a child respond in your class is to have a good relationship with that student. Speak with your students often on a one-to-one basis, so they will feel comfortable speaking to you during class as well. And always listen! Remember that your classroom should be a place of safety, acceptance, and encouragement.

How do I get kids to remember the lesson?

Children will remember what they experience. To remember a Bible lesson, kids need to experience the sights, sounds, smells, tastes, and tangible aspects of it.

● *Bring the Bible to life.* To teach the story of Jonah, you may want to gather in a cold, dark classroom, Open cans of sardines or tuna and turn on a fan. Then spray kids with water from a spray bottle or squirt gun for effect as you tell the story. Or consider having kids sit in a box shaped like an ark as you tell them about Noah and they listen to animal sounds on a cassette. You might play a game in your class to find the lost coin as you study Luke 15:8-10, have a Passover feast when you study Luke 22:7-38, or march around a pile of blocks that you pretend is the city of Jericho when you study Joshua 5-6. Anything you can do to make the lesson real for the children will help them to remember the story.

● *Use key phrases.* Repeat important words and phrases over and over again as the story unfolds. If the children hear the same exact phrase again and again, they'll relate it to the story. Choose a word or phrase that will link the story to its application. For example, when you tell the story of Noah's Ark, keep reminding the children that God keeps his promises. Everything you do during the class time should reinforce this one concept. At the end of class, you can be certain that the kids will know what you've taught.

● **Do class projects.** Children remember when they're involved in interesting projects. Instead of telling kids how big the ark was, measure it out in the church parking lot. Turn your classroom into a tabernacle. Teach children how to write their names in Hebrew. Practice making matzo bread in eighteen minutes or less as Jewish people do, to make sure the bread has no time to rise.

● **Practice what you learn.** Children will remember lessons they learn when they're given an opportunity to practice what they've learned. For example, if you've taught the children to be generous with their possessions like the widow who gave all she had, have a toy drive and encourage the children to give some of their toys to kids who need them. Or you might practice encouragement by sending letters to elderly church members. You could practice joy by having a party. Always tie the project back to the Bible lesson.

How do I develop spiritual leadership in children?

C hildren and teens have a lot to offer where ministry is concerned. If children begin serving early, and if they have positive experiences, they'll most likely continue some form of service when they are older. These ideas can help develop leadership skills in your kids:

● **Give kids responsibilities during meeting times.** Encourage children to learn leadership skills by having them lead small parts of regular meeting times such as Sunday school or children's church. Children can easily take on individual roles such as prayer leader, usher, or treasurer. It also works well to have small groups of children working on committees. For example, you might form a group of four to five older children to be the worship team for children's church. This group would work with an adult helper to choose and lead music during children's church.

As children become accustomed to leading, give them larger leadership roles, such as directing a skit or helping coordinate transportation to a service project. Always make sure that an adult is ultimately in charge. However, the adult's main role should be helping the children learn how to lead.

● **Involve kids in small groups.** Older elementary children and young teens can begin to develop spiritual leadership in small groups or classes. Children can be encouraged to lead prayer times and discussion times in these groups. They can also coordinate whose house the group will meet at, who will bring the treats, and who will notify the others when plans must change. As always, an adult should ultimately be in charge, but should help the children take on as much responsibility as they can.

● **Involve kids in teaching younger kids.** Older children make great teaching assistants because younger children often respect and admire them. Older kids work well as VBS assistants, Sunday school assistants, and preschool and nursery helpers. Make sure children know what you expect of them. Working with younger children is a position of trust and responsibility—not an excuse to get out of church. If you use older children as helpers in the nursery, be sure they know they are expected to care for the babies rather than talk with their friends. Make sure they know safety rules and understand what tasks only adults are allowed to do. For example, you may want to make a rule that only adults will change diapers. Encourage your young assistants to tell the younger kids about God.

● **Involve kids in church life.** Children can be involved in all kinds of projects within the church. They can serve as greeters at the door on Sunday mornings, and they can go with an adult to call on visitors later in the week. Children can help the custodian clean the building, and they can bake cookies for shut-ins. Children can help fold bulletins, and they can provide special music. Children can help serve a meal for senior adults, and they can collect supplies for missionaries.

Look around your church for opportunities for children to serve. They'll learn that being a spiritual leader means serving the body of Christ. You'll learn that every child has something to offer.

How do I make sure kids learn what they need to know about God?

There are two important components to making sure kids know what they need to know about God. First, you must have a plan in place. Second, you have to be able to determine whether you met the goals of your plan by seeing what the kids have actually learned.

● **The plan.** Your church needs to have a comprehensive plan for the children's ministry. This plan will spell out what Bible stories and concepts are covered at what age and how often you'll repeat the stories and concepts. Most likely, the children's pastor or coordinator has already looked into this issue. Talk to the children's pastor or coordinator at your church, and find out what concepts you need to stress in the age level you teach. You'll probably cover the points that your church feels are important for your age level by teaching the lessons as they come in the curriculum your church uses. If each teacher in your church is in charge of choosing a curriculum for his or her class, you'll need to create a curriculum planning committee to go over your plans and objectives to make sure that kids don't cover the same Bible stories every year.

● **What the kids learn.** Figuring out what kids have learned in Sunday school can be tough. In schools, kids are regularly tested, but tests probably won't go over too well in most Sunday school classes. Instead, focus on review.

Ask questions that build on previous lessons. For example, when you're studying how Moses responded to God's command to talk to Pharaoh, you might review the story of Abraham by asking the children to compare Moses' response to God and Abraham's response to God's command that he move away from his home. Ask questions about the lessons from previous weeks. Ask children what they remember from last week. Ask children who their favorite Bible character is and why.

Another way to assess how kids are learning is to observe their behavior. If you've been teaching about kindness, watch to see how kind the children behave to each other. If you've been teaching about prayer, find out how the kids are using that information in their lives. How is God answering their prayers? What are they learning about God through spending more time with him.

Quick Relief for
Teaching
the Bible

How do I get kids to have a quiet time?

Developing a personal devotion time is a tough discipline no matter what your age. But even young children can benefit from a regular time of prayer and Bible study. These ideas will help you guide children in this practice:

● **Help kids understand that God wants a relationship with them.** Children need to know that being a Christian is more than knowing Bible stories and understanding right from wrong. They need to see that being a Christian means having a deep relationship with God. That relationship grows just as a friendship does—by spending quality time together. Essentially, that's what a quiet time or devotion time provides—a chance to spend time with God, sharing our fears, concerns, hopes, and dreams.

● **Model a quiet time with Christ.** If you don't already have a regular devotion time, begin right away. Talk to the kids about your time with God. It's OK to share how you struggle to make it consistent. Share your struggles and also share the benefits of becoming closer to God. One Sunday school teacher began to have a personal quiet time with God when he was in high school. That experience helped him make a habit of reading through the Bible each year. Then he explained to his Sunday school students how he structured his quiet time. This teacher explained that he kept a Quiet Time Diary where he logged (1) a passage of Scripture he was reading, (2) a brief description of the passage, and (3) a summary of how it applies to his life. He began his Scripture reading with a prayer: "Lord, please open up my eyes to understand what the Scripture is saying to me today!" Showing kids how it's done is always more powerful than telling kids to do it!

● **Give kids encouragement.** Part of our role as Christian teachers is to show kids how to have a quiet time and to teach them about the benefits. But a bigger job may be encouraging kids to stick with it. To have a regular quiet time is a discipline. Do all you can to encourage kids without making them feel guilty if they aren't ready for a quiet time or if they don't want to do it every day.

● **Give kids freedom.** Realize that God created us all to be different. Help children realize that they can have their devotion time just before bed or just before heading off to school. A devotion time might be studying a passage of Scripture, but it can also be praising God for his creation while you walk to school. Scripture reading could consist of one verse or one chapter—it might even be remembering verses that have already been memorized. Prayer can be written down, spoken quietly, or painted on canvas. Quiet times can be done every day or on Monday, Wednesday, and Friday. What counts is getting close to God and doing it often.

● **Ask kids how they are doing.** This is a great way to help children become comfortable talking about their relationships with God. Provide a time for kids to share what God is doing in their lives or what they learned from their devotion time. But be sure that this experience doesn't make kids feel guilty if they haven't had a devotion time. Ask kids who are doing their quiet time to share their successes. Soon you will develop a culture of acceptance and expectation that speaks powerfully to all children.

How do I help kids stand for God even if they have to stand alone?

Peer pressure is a big deal for kids. It's tough to stand for God when your friends and classmates don't. These ideas can help you encourage children to give their allegiance to God:

● **Secure, confident kids stand for God.** Making a decision to stand for God when your peers are going against God is a mark of maturity that many adults haven't developed. We can help kids stand for God by grounding them in their faith and encouraging them to be confident in themselves and confident in God. We ground kids in their faith by teaching what the Bible says and by teaching how to discern right from wrong. We can help kids be confident in themselves by allowing them to grow and succeed and by giving them an accurate picture of who they are in Christ. A teacher's praise, encouragement, love, and acceptance helps kids gain confidence. Kids learn to be confident in God as they discover God's strength and faithfulness, and understand that they can rely on God every day.

● **Kids need to be shown how.** Standing for God means going against the flow. We need to show kids what this looks like in everyday life. Standing for God means treating someone with a disability with compassion and love. It means studying hard and not cheating on a test. It means resisting the crowd that wants to mock and poke fun at someone who doesn't play very well on the playground.

Kids need to know how to stand up for their beliefs in a way that will bring glory to God—not with a "holier than thou" attitude. Instead, standing for God should be a natural outcome as we strive to be people of character and integrity. We help children become people of character and integrity when we encourage them to make right choices and to guard their thoughts.

How do I encourage kids to become disciples—to know, love, and obey God?

Accoring to Matthew 28:19, the main goal of our teaching is to make disciples. The fact is that we as teachers have a child for only one year of his or her life, making our job much more urgent, if not impossible, to complete. Here are some practical ways we can encourage children to know, love, and obey God:

● **Establish clear objectives for your time with all your children.** It may be trying to memorize certain verses, or understanding key Bible stories, or simply to experience God in a personal way each week. Whatever your goal, set one and make sure you have achieved it.

● **Be enthusiastic about Jesus Christ.** Have a passion for Christ that infects the kids. Show that he is the most important part of your life.

● **Set an example yourself.** Be a growing learner who hungers and thirsts after righteousness. Be vulnerable and transparent. Let your students see you grow.

● **Give kids the freedom to fail.** Let kids know by your patience with them, your hopeful expectations, and your positive warmth toward them that God will never give up on them.

● **Tell stories of disciples.** Let kids know that the stories in Scripture are true and not made-up. People who depended on God, believed in God, and lived to please him are all significant models.

How do I teach kids how to study the Bible?

Studying the Bible is a skill that will benefit children their entire lives. Here are some ideas to help you teach children to study God's Word:

- **Model it.** Passionately, enthusiastically, and practically make the Bible part of who you are. Carry it with you, memorize it, consult it often, and let your students know that you are obedient to it.

- **Use the Bible.** Keep your Bible in your hands or nearby throughout the lesson. Let the children see you referring to it as you tell the story. Read verses from the Bible, not from the teacher's guide. Let the Bible be the ultimate authority in your class.

- **Make Scripture interesting.** Use teaching techniques such as drama and role-play to bring the past into the present. Explain unusual Bible customs, serve Bible-time food, and explain and enjoy the imagery of Bible poetry.

- **Choose age-appropriate passages.** Nothing quells a child's enthusiasm for learning like trying to teach a lesson that's too hard or too easy. Get to know the kids in your classroom, and adapt the Bible lesson to their age level. Also, use an age-appropriate Bible translation so kids won't struggle over difficult words. Older elementary kids may enjoy comparing several different translations of Scripture and discussing why translators chose to use different words.

- **Get children to dig in and find answers for themselves.** It probably will never occur to kids to read the Bible unless they are introduced to reading it. Whenever possible, have children look up passages themselves. Make sure they understand how the Bible is organized—that sixty-six smaller books make up the Bible. Make sure they know what chapter and verse numbers mean. Then help them understand what the Bible is saying to them. Teach them how God's Word applies to their lives.

- **Explain difficult passages.** Even Peter said that some of Paul's writings "contain some things that are hard to understand" (2 Peter 3:16). Study the tough passages before introducing them to children. You may even want to consult a Bible commentary. Then help children understand what is being said in the passage. Make these verses come alive in new ways for children.

- **Teach that God's Word is important and eternal.** Kids won't know that God's Word is more important than any other book unless we tell them. Treat the Bible with respect. Explain that the Bible is true and that it will last forever. Help children understand that the Bible tells how God has worked through history to bring people into relationship with him. Help the children see that it's important to respect the Bible and its teachings.

- **Encourage children to read the Bible on their own.** Do everything you can to ensure that every child has an age-appropriate Bible at home. Explain that it's important to know what God says and that the Bible is God's message to us. You might want to give children fun, easy, and non-threatening "homework" assignments that require kids to look in their Bibles. For example, kids love trivia questions. You might ask a question such as, "When in the Bible did an animal talk and what did it say?" Then guide them to the book of Numbers and let them hunt for the answer.

How can I help kids develop a strong prayer life so they'll feel comfortable praying out loud?

Teachers can do several things to make prayer an important part of children's lives:

- **Teach the purpose of prayer.** Kids may say the purpose of prayer is to ask for things they want. Help children get a more accurate picture of the purpose of prayer by explaining that we pray so that we can know God and what he wants for us.

- **Make God real to kids.** It's uncomfortable to have a seemingly one-sided conversation with someone you know nothing about. Kids won't want to talk to God until they feel that they know God and are close to him. Make God real in your classroom by emphasizing his role in the Bible stories you teach. Emphasize God's character and personality so that kids are familiar with who God is.

- **Praying out loud isn't for everyone.** How we pray is not as important as our attitude when we pray. Let a child develop a heart for God instead of developing good public-speaking skills. God looks at the attitude of our heart as he listens to our prayers.

● *Begin and end class with prayer.* One Sunday school teacher made a habit of praying throughout her lesson. If a student had an "owie," she would stop to pray. This teacher showed her students that prayer should be a part of our very existence. By praying for her students, this teacher showed her love for them in a tangible way.

● *Have a kids' prayer breakfast or "day of prayer."* Spend one Sunday morning a month to take a few minutes to concentrate just on prayer. Have a continental breakfast and pray in a circle, in small groups, in unison, or just quietly.

● *Have kids keep a prayer calendar or journal.* Encourage kids to document answers to prayer including positive, negative, or "wait" answers.

● *Pray for current issues.* Pray simply and clearly for the events of everyday life and events in the news. This shows children that God cares about everything that happens in our world.

How do I spark a passionate love for God in children?

Love for God springs from our relationship with God. Children have a natural inclination to trust, connect, love, and be concerned for others. Tapping into that innate desire is the key to getting kids to love God. Use these ideas to help kids develop a passion for God:

● *Communicate your love for God.* Children learn through our lives and actions, so let your love for God shine through. Share how God has shown his grace and goodness to you. Share the ways God has answered your prayers. Make your love for God evident in all you do.

● *Show them God's power in the Bible.* As you teach Bible stories, emphasize that God was always working to bring people into relationships with him. Show instances of God's love and mercy. Point out that what you read in the Bible is true. Make God real and alive.

● *Tell about God's character.* Let children get to know God and his attributes. Explain that God is infinite; eternal; unchangeable; and full of love, kindness, and goodness. It might be best to explain these attributes by showing children how

God dealt with the people in the Bible. The Bible shows us God's character through his actions.

● **Tell kids over and over how much God cares for them.** Unconditional love, acceptance, and grace are powerful concepts that are unique to the Christian faith. Tell children that God made us and loves us. Tell children that God sent Jesus to forgive our sins. Tell them that God is gracious and his lovingkindness is eternal.

● **Bring in guests who can demonstrate a passionate love for God.** Every week some churches invite a member of their congregation to share with children. These people tell the story of how they each came to know Christ personally, including all the troubles and trials that led them to trust God. What a great way to teach kids what love for God looks like.

How do I teach kids about the scary or violent aspects of the Bible?

irst, realize that children don't need to hear ALL the scary and violent details of the Bible. In many ways, the Bible is an adult book. Many of its stories and themes are tough for adults to understand. We need to be careful that what we teach children is appropriate.

● **Focus on age-appropriate details of any Bible story.** Consider the story of David and Goliath. While fourth- and fifth-graders might be able to handle the entire story (com-

THE LATEST IN THE EVER-EXPANDING ARRAY OF CHRISTIAN PRODUCTS.

plete with David cutting off Goliath's head), it may not be wise to share that information with four- and five-year-olds. With preschoolers, it's enough to teach them that David was brave, that God helped him fight a mean giant, and that God protected David from the giant. You'll find that with young children, there are stories that you probably won't want to tell at all, such as the story of David and Bathsheba.

● *Focus on positive truths in each story.* No matter what you're teaching, it's always best to find a positive lesson that you'd like the children to learn. Let that positive message be your lesson focus. For example, in the story of Cain and Abel, you might teach that God wants us to treat others with love. In the story of David and Goliath, you might teach that God is stronger than any enemy. Remember that it's never enough for us to teach just the facts of a Bible story. Our purpose is to help children know, love, and obey God. That purpose is best achieved when we explain the positive truths in each Bible story.

● *Know which details are important.* Depending on the story, the violent or scary aspects may not be relevant to the point you'd like to make. For example, in the story of Jesus' death and resurrection, even children need to know that Jesus was beaten, mistreated, and killed, to pay for our sins. But it might not be necessary to tell all the gruesome details of the crucifixion. Again, focus on the main truth of the story and what is most important for the children to learn and understand.

How do I help kids learn to discern right from wrong—and then choose to do right?

This is a tough one. *Knowing* right from wrong is relatively easy to teach. But teaching children to *choose* to do right involves shaping their hearts and their consciences—it requires a sensitivity to the Holy Spirit and a desire to obey God. Here are some ideas:

● *Cover the basics.* Be intentional about teaching children the difference between right and wrong. Don't assume that they know that lying is always wrong or that stealing is always wrong. Relative morality is very much accepted in our culture these days. Our culture teaches that right and wrong are determined by the situation a person is in. The Bible teaches that wrong things are always wrong.

● **Tell children why.** Don't forget to explain why stealing is wrong and why envy is wrong. We want to train children to *discern* right from wrong. It's not always easy to decide what is right and what is wrong. When kids get into tough situations, we want them to be able to use critical-thinking skills to determine what to do. That means that kids need to know the "why's" behind the rules.

● **Teach children about consequences.** The rules that God gives us are designed to keep us safe and full of joy. When we follow God's rules for right and wrong, we are able to live the kind of abundant life that God promises for those who love him. Teach children that following God's rules leads us to good things. Breaking the rules or choosing to do wrong brings painful consequences and sorrow.

● **Give them opportunities to practice making good choices.** Use techniques such as debate, role-play, and discussion groups to give children time to think about what choices they'd make. The more practice they have in class, the easier it'll be for them to actually do the right thing in real life. Cover as many situations as you can. Children need to know how to apply the large, general concepts they learn to the small events that make up each day.

● **Teach kids to love God.** As Christians, the reason we want to do right is that we want to please God. Offer opportunities in your classroom for children to meet with God and develop a relationship with God. When children learn to love God with a deep, abiding love, they'll be motivated to do the right thing out of devotion to God.

How do I establish Christian values and commitment in children from non-Christian families?

Even when these children spend time at church, they spend a lot more time at home in a non-Christian setting. It can be tough to encourage Christian values and commitment to

"The Lord caused me to lie down in green pastures once, and I got in big trouble for getting grass stains on my good clothes."

take root and grow when there may be a great deal of non-Christian influence the rest of the week.

However, you must also realize what a wonderful opportunity you have when a child from a non-Christian family attends your class. Many times the shining example of a young child who loves God can influence an entire family to give their lives to God. Here are some things you can do as you teach these children:

● **Be sure you cover the basics.** Sometimes we assume that the children in our classes have heard all the Bible stories a dozen times. Children from non-Christian families probably don't know many stories. These children may not want to let on that they don't know the story because of fear that they will look ignorant in front of everyone else. Cover each Bible subject in complete detail to make sure everyone knows the facts.

● **Repeat important theological facts.** For example, make it a repetitive theme in your class that God loves each person. Repeat over and over why Jesus died on the cross, how we find forgiveness for our sins, and how we gain eternal life. You'd be surprised how many kids never understand these basic theological ideas—even kids who've been in church their entire lives.

● **Explain the reasons behind Christian moral values.** From an outsider's point of view, Christianity can look like a random set of restrictive do's and don'ts. It's not enough to tell kids that lying is always wrong. We also have to teach children that truth and honesty are Christlike characteristics. When we are honest with others, we are imitating our God, and we are showing respect for ourselves and others.

● **_Focus on positives._** Upon being introduced to Christianity, too many children are turned off because they're reprimanded too often and too harshly for unChristlike behavior. They grow up thinking God is harsh, angry, and punitive. That's not what we want children to learn about God. Instead of expecting children to act like mature Christians, realize that Christian growth is a slow process. Encourage children for the good things they do. Gently correct young Christians when they make wrong choices.

● **_Use this opportunity to bring God into children's homes._** Visit children and meet their families. Let the families know how much you care for their children. Hold nonthreatening events that bring families to church. Parents love to see their children perform. Invite families to attend dramas and music events. You may also want to hold family events such as picnics or holiday dinners. Use these events as a chance to make friends instead of feeling compelled to present the Gospel right away. Non-Christian families may feel threatened if you preach at them. These families need to see the church as a place where they'll be accepted and loved.

Quick Relief for
Relationships

How do I deal with a child I don't like?

When you work with people, it's very natural to occasionally come across people, even children, you don't like. However, God calls us to love and care for all people. Here are some things you can do to get beyond your dislike:

● **Come to terms with your own attitude and emotions.** Try to understand why you dislike the child. You may find that your dislike is really only discomfort because the child is different from you. For example, a quiet, introverted person may find a highly active child annoying. When you examine your feelings, you may also find that the child reminds you of negative traits you had as a child. By understanding your own attitude and emotions, you may find that your negative feelings lessen in intensity.

Also, looking into your own attitude can mature your understanding of God's grace and unconditional love. Consider how deeply God loves each person on earth regardless of how annoying, sinful, or unlovable we are. Try to see each child through God's eyes and treat him or her as God would.

● **Get to know what is important, significant, and unique about that child.** Seeing the good in a child whose behavior is rotten can be difficult. However, their behavior (what they do or don't do) stands in stark contrast with who they are (unique and special creations of God's). It takes time to find something special about a child you don't care for. When you do, though, focus on that.

One teacher had a terrible time with a child who always arrived early. Jimmy really seemed to enjoy making the orderly classroom look like a pie factory after a Three Stooges' visit. The teacher was frustrated. Finally, in a desperate attempt to minimize the damage, he asked Jimmy to help set out the crayons and papers. To the teacher's amazement, Jimmy eagerly agreed to help. The teacher was successful that day because he took energy that was being focused inappropriately and gave it direction, order, and purpose. It turned out that Jimmy was special because of his energy level and his willingness to help. When the teacher discovered this, Jimmy thrived, the teacher lost a huge source of frustration, and the teacher grew to like and appreciate Jimmy.

● **Treat children with equal respect, dignity, and love.**
Love children for who they are; like them for who they will
become. Treat children according to their potential rather
than how they deserve to be treated right now. Because all
children were created by God, they all have the potential to
lead lives that are pleasing to God. Children know if you
don't like them. When children sense your dislike, you lose
the ability to positively influence them. Instead of giving negative attention or no attention to children we don't like, be
respectful of their individuality. When you need to correct,
do so with as much gentleness as you can, realizing that
each child is loved by God.

● **Know that they will grow!** Children will change and become different next year, three years from now, and five years
from now. One teacher had a group of two-year-olds who
were difficult to deal with. Other teachers dreaded the time
when those children were scheduled to be "graduated" into
their rooms. For three years the word was out on these kids'
behavior. Sure enough, the group kept up its reckless behavior.
Then they were promoted into the five-year-old class. The
teachers in that class all resigned because they didn't want to
deal with those "wild kids." A whole new team of teachers was
recruited. That team didn't know they were getting those "terrible two's" who were now "five's." Because the teachers didn't
expect them to be difficult, the kids didn't act difficult. Kids
change if we allow them.

How do I deal with kids who have ADD or ADHD?

Unless you've read a lot about Attention Deficit Disorder
(ADD) and Attention Deficit Hyperactivity Disorder
(ADHD) or have had experience with a child who has it, it can
be tough to understand the challenges these kids face. Understanding how this disorder affects children will help you know
how to teach them.

In one church, a doctor described his son's struggle with
ADHD before the boy began to use medication. The boy had
difficulty organizing work and gave the impression that he
hadn't heard instructions. He was easily distracted; made
careless, impulsive errors; frequently interrupted in class; had   **53**

difficulty waiting for his turn; and failed to follow through on teacher or parent requests.

"In effect, he was receiving information overload," the doctor said. "Sitting here in your office, do you hear the noise of the air conditioner? Do you hear your heart beating? Do you notice that you are breathing in a regular pattern? Do you notice that people are speaking softly outside? A child with ADD or ADHD hears and notices all of these at the same time. They are overstimulated and in need of focus. I have recommended prescription drugs for years because it deadens those noises that other people can tune out automatically."

Here are some things that a teacher should and should not do with an ADD/ADHD child:

● **Do not try to diagnose a child.** This can be done only by a physician. A comprehensive plan of treatment includes ongoing evaluation by a qualified physician and, often, medical psychotherapy for the child, help for the family, and consultation with teachers. What you can give parents is your prayerful support and affirmation.

● **Do not make children with ADD or ADHD stand out or set them apart from the rest of the class.** Treat them as you would other children in your class. They are to be equally enjoyed and affirmed.

● **Encourage parents to consult with their doctor about continuing the child's medication on the weekends.** Some physicians prefer that kids take a break from medication over the weekends. But this merely intensifies their problems at church and can cause children to feel unsuccessful and unfocused in a place where you want them to focus on God's grace.

● **Consult with parents to make the child's church experience successful.** Parents know what works with their children. Most parents are ahead of the game in providing a successful learning environment for their children. Ask parents what you can do to help their child enjoy church and learn to love God.

● **Adjust the learning environment.** Is there too much stimulation (both verbally and visually) so that the child cannot focus? Try to minimize distractions. Also realize that children with ADD and ADHD may need to move more than other children. If your class times focus on sitting and listening types of activities, consider adding more action. Including movement activities can actually help kids learn. Transitions can be tough for these kids. Try a variety of activities and find out what works best. Then develop a classroom routine and stick with it. It can also help to give the child a "buddy" to minimize social isolation or abandonment. A friend can do a lot to keep a child with ADD on track.

● **Consider limiting the class size.** You can give special attention to children with special needs if you are not concerned with a large group of children. Talk with your children's director or pastor and work together to make the classroom setting and size the best it can be.

● **Educate yourself with material that allows you to understand both children and their families.** A great resource is *You & Your ADD Child*. Dr. Paul Warren and Jody Capehart encourage teachers to provide an environment that allows for exploration and limited distractions. ADD requires children to be less verbal and more experiential. Use activities that rely on experience rather than rote types of teaching. Also, each time you teach find something good that the child accomplished and use it to encourage the parent and child.

There are so many kids in my class — how do I make time to build a relationship with each one?

Unless you have a really small class, it's nearly impossible to develop significant relationships with kids through class alone. Use these ideas to build relationships both before and after class:

Before Class

● Pray specifically for each child. When you are focused on praying for a child, the crowd diminishes to one individual with many needs. Let the children know that you are praying for them.

● Arrive early to greet those who do come early. You can't give personal attention to everyone, but during this brief period before the "crowd" arrives, you can get to know some children better.

● Speak to kids' parents as they drop off their children. Getting to know parents will help you understand their children.

PORTLOCK

"I think we have everything; paper plates, soda, cold cuts, chips, dips, candy, napkins, hot dogs, hamburgers...oops! I forgot to invite the kids."

It also opens the door to phone calls, letters, or personal visits later.

After Class

● Schedule social times with children at one of their homes.

● Invite a child's family to dinner.

● Write to children who missed class telling them that you noticed they were not in class and that you hope they will come back next week.

● Write to kids on their birthdays or when they accomplish something significant (honor roll, graduation, recitals, ball games, etc.).

● Attend children's sporting events, plays, and other special events.

● Spend time visiting kids who are in the hospital.

● Send small gifts at Christmas.

Our church is having trouble— we may even split! How can I help the children during this struggle?

When a church is involved in a serious problem, the children can't help but be aware. And chances are, they're scared and confused by all the fighting and discord. In many ways a church split affects children like a divorce. That's why it's important to be as supportive and encouraging as possible. Here are some tips to help you help the children:

- **Don't get involved in the fight.** Many church disagreements concern matters that aren't of the utmost importance to every church member. Unless the issue is theological, biblical, or moral, stay out of the disagreement in order to help the children you are guiding and teaching. If the issues are serious, either leave the church or stay, pray, and be positive.

- **Answer questions and offer comfort.** If children are aware of the problem, address their concerns in class. Even young children can sense when people aren't getting along, and they may ask questions about what's going on. Answer these questions as honestly and positively as possible. Explain that sometimes grownups disagree and get angry. But emphasize that God is pleased when we love each other and treat each other with kindness. Tell the children it's sad that people don't always get along. Reassure them that even though the adults may be angry with each other, they all want what's best for the church and for the children. You may even want to let children pray for the church.

- **Focus on learning.** As much as possible, keep the children in your classroom focused on God, the Bible, and the lesson. No matter what results from the church disagreement, use your time with kids to its best advantage. Help them to see church as a place of warmth, caring, and learning about God. Do everything you can to create an atmosphere of fun learning.

Disciplining kids makes me feel like a tyrant when I'd rather show them love. How do I get kids to behave?

Begin by realizing that children need and want boundaries. They also want respect and the ability to make their own choices. You can show love by helping children understand what is and is not appropriate behavior. Initially the task will be difficult, but in the end the rewards will be great.

- **Set rules.** Start by determining what the rules of your classroom will be. Depending on the age of the students in your class, you may need to make this decision. If you have older children, work with them to determine the boundaries so that they've had input into what'll be expected of them. Keep the list of rules simple, and keep it posted. With younger children you may want to use pictures. Consider what you expect of the students. How will they act toward you? How will they treat others? How will they use the materials and supplies? The shorter the list of rules, the easier it will be to remember them later on. Phrase your list in a positive way. Rather than saying, "Don't talk when others are talking," say, "Respect others by listening while they talk."

● **Determine what the discipline or consequences will be for not following the rules.** Will there be a warning first? Will there be a timeout? How many times will children be reminded of the rules or put in a timeout before their parents are contacted? Having a plan in place will help you know a procedure to follow in each situation. This plan will help you to be fair and consistent with each student.

A discipline plan keeps you from feeling as frustrated, frazzled, or furious as you would without a plan. Any time you lose control and raise your voice, the child has won and has learned what buttons to push. Rather than letting a discipline problem escalate to that level, simply remind the child that he or she is responsible for his or her own actions. If a child chooses not to follow the rules, then the child must accept the consequences. Make sure you're prepared to follow through with the discipline.

● **Partner with parents.** Don't forget that God has made parents responsible for training their children. You'll have a child for only a couple hours each week, and it's very difficult to teach appropriate behavior in that short time. Communicate with parents constantly about their child's progress, both in spiritual growth and classroom behavior. And don't take it personally if a child misbehaves. Remember that we all have a sinful nature, and children are still learning how to control their behavior.

If you have already gone through this process and are following your discipline plan diligently, but you are still having discipline problems, here are a few more ideas:

● Involve the parents as classroom helpers. Set up a "parent of the week" program, and ask that each parent take a turn. Having a parent in class tends to quell a child's desire to act out.

● Use positive reinforcement. If there's a group of children who are causing trouble, recruit the ringleader to help out in the classroom. He or she can come early to help set up or stay late to clean up. Sometimes the positive attention you give reduces the desire for negative attention.

● Make contracts. A contract with your students can also be helpful, especially with older elementary children. Write down the rules of the contract. Be specific about what you expect and what they expect. Include what the rewards will be for following the rules and what the consequences will be for breaking the rules.

Our kids come from two schools, and they stay in cliques. How can I create a more tightknit group?

This problem will take a while to solve. It takes time and consistent attention to help kids make new friends, instead of interacting solely with the friends they've already made in another setting.

● *Concentrate on whole-group activities.* Some of your attention should go toward creating a "class consciousness." This means that your class should feel an identity or a cohesiveness. You can create this identity by planning activities and projects that the whole group works on together. For example, if your crew enjoys music, you might come up with a class song and develop motions that go with it. Your group may discover that they all share tender feelings for the senior adults in your church. Create group identity by working together to serve the older adults in your church.

● *Concentrate on small-group activities.* A lot of attention needs to go toward small groups. Of course, you must arrange the groups so that cliques don't stay together. These small groups can be formed for discussion, for projects, for games, for service projects, for midweek Bible studies or for social events. Small groups are great vehicles for making friends. It's important that you give the children time to really get to know each other in small groups, so plan several opportunities for kids to meet in the same small group. However, you don't want to form new cliques, so mix up the groups every once in a while. For example, you might want to form new small groups every quarter.

● **Concentrate on fun.** Kids won't have a chance to make new friends if your class time is structured so tightly that they never have time to mingle and chat. Be purposeful about providing time to have fun. You don't have to sacrifice your teaching goals to have fun—learning activities can be fun and still provide time for interaction. For example, you might involve the children in making a model of the tower of Babel or play a game about Noah's ark. Be mindful of who the children interact with during a lesson. If they interact only with you, they won't ever make new friends. Encourage children to interact with each other by including pair-shares. Pair-shares are discussion questions that children discuss with a partner. You'll also want to plan for fun times apart from the church. Invite children to a pizza party or a pool party. Take everyone bowling or to the roller rink. Skate to the park for a picnic, or go for a hike in a state park. Have fun together, and kids will make new friends.

Some kids are downright mean. How can I encourage them to be kind?

When you look at the sweet, angelic faces of children, it's easy to expect that their actions will match up with their looks. But children struggle with character flaws just as adults do. To encourage children to be kind, we must first honestly recognize that sometimes children can be hurtful. We must also recognize that children have a great ability to be empathetic, caring people. It's our job to help them learn how to act on their feelings of kindness rather than their impulses or hurtfulness.

● **Make Luke 6:31 your class motto.** "Do unto others" is a concept that's easily understood, even by young children. Post the verse on the door and walls of your classroom. Recite the verse together. Remind children that God is pleased when you treat others the way you want to be treated.

● **Model kindness.** In all of your dealings with children, be gentle, kind, respectful, and straightforward. If we honor sarcasm, children will honor it. If we honor mean-spirited jokes, children will honor them. If we respond to children in anger, children will respond to each other with anger. Set the tone for your classroom with your warmth and caring. Encourage the children to behave in the same way.

● *Respond enthusiastically to children's kind acts.* Children would much rather be recognized for doing something well than be reprimanded for messing up. Often, children with a tendency for mean behavior will act up just to get your attention, even if it's negative attention. By reprimanding them, you're actually encouraging them to act up more. Instead, ignore their bad behavior as much as possible and gush over their attempts to be kind.

How do I involve loners?

We must strive to make every child feel comfortable, accepted, and loved in church. The activities we plan should always be inclusive—we want to bring kids into the circle of Christian fellowship. However, it's also important to remember that each child is an individual with different needs and interests. Some children are loners because they haven't figured out how to fit in. Other children are loners because they prefer to do activities on their own. Sometimes our job is to help loners find friendships in the group. Sometimes our job is to respect a child's need for time alone. Here are some things you can do to make your class a comfortable place for all children:

● *Get to know the children.* Make friends with the children. Know who their parents are, how many brothers and sisters they have, and where they go to school. The more effort you expend in making friends with your children, the more comfortable they'll feel in class. Children who know their teacher likes them tend to become more involved in the class.

● *Include activities that help children know each other.* With young children, this can be as easy as playing a simple Get-to-know-you game where children learn each other's names. With older children, you can have parties and more sophisticated games where children compare their interests and abilities.

● *Include activities that interest different kinds of learners.* Do you remember what it was like in school to be expected to participate in classes and activities you weren't good at? Some kids become loners because they're embarrassed by their lack of ability. Some kids can't carry a tune—it's tough for them if you plan too many music activities. Some kids are slow readers. If most of your class time involves reading aloud, these kids will be left behind. Find out what excites your children. Plan lots of different kinds of activities that interest lots of different kinds of kids.

● **Respect that sometimes kids don't want to be involved.** You may never know what happened to a child before he or she came to your class. Maybe a pet died or a parent was angry. It could be that this child got a bad grade in math or had a fight with his or her best friend. Sometimes kids feel sad or out of sorts. As adults, we can decide not to go to an event when we're feeling especially down, but children don't usually have that freedom. They go where their parents take them. Sometimes kids need a little bit of space to deal with negative emotions.

● **Be sensitive to children who haven't yet developed good social skills.** Some children may not be around other children a lot. They have no siblings, or they may live in mostly-adult neighborhoods. Some kids just aren't natural friend-makers. Gently encourage them to get involved with the class. Pair them with children who are particularly kind. But also realize that teaching these children how to make friends can be a slow process.

● **Include activities in which children work together in small groups.** Create small discussion groups or have children work in teams to complete a project. Build into the activity various roles that will guide the children into working together. For example, in a discussion group, one child can be the question reader, one child can be the encourager, and one child can be the cheerleader. In a project team, one child can be the supply-getter, one child can be the direction-reader, and one child can be the trouble-shooter.

Group Publishing, Inc.
Attention: Product Development
P.O. Box 481
Loveland, CO 80539
Fax: (970) 669-1994

Evaluation for
QUICK RELIEF FOR SUNDAY SCHOOL TEACHERS

Please help Group Publishing, Inc., continue to provide innovative and useful resources for ministry. Please take a moment to fill out this evaluation and mail or fax it to us. Thanks!

● ● ●

1. As a whole, this book has been (circle one)

not very helpful   very helpful

1   2   3   4   5   6   7   8   9   10

2. The best things about this book:

3. Ways this book could be improved:

4. Things I will change because of this book:

5. Other books I'd like to see Group publish in the future:

6. Would you be interested in field-testing future Group products and giving us your feedback? If so, please fill in the information below:

Name _____

Street Address _____

City _____ State_____ Zip _____

Phone Number _____ Date _____

Group's
hands-On
BiBLE
curriculum

BRING THE BIBLE TO LIFE FOR YOUR 1ST- THROUGH 6TH-GRADERS...
WITH GROUP'S HANDS-ON BIBLE CURRICULUM™
Energize your kids with Active Learning!

Group's **Hands-On Bible Curriculum**™ will help you teach the Bible in a radical new way. It's based on Active Learning—the same teaching method Jesus used.

In each lesson, students will participate in exciting and memorable learning experiences using fascinating gadgets and gizmos you've not seen with any other curriculum. Your elementary students will discover biblical truths and <u>remember</u> what they learn because they're <u>doing</u> instead of just listening.

You'll save time and money, too!

While students are learning more, you'll be working less—simply follow the quick and easy instructions in the **Teacher Guide**. You'll get tons of material for an energy-packed 35- to 60-minute lesson. And, if you have extra time, there's an arsenal of Bonus Ideas and Time Stuffers to keep kids occupied—and learning! Plus, you'll SAVE BIG over other curriculum programs that require you to buy expensive separate student books—all student handouts in Group's **Hands-On Bible Curriculum** are photocopiable!

In addition to the easy-to-use **Teacher Guide**, you'll get all the essential teaching materials you need in a ready-to-use **Learning Lab**®. No more running from store to store hunting for lesson materials—all the active-learning tools you need to teach 13 exciting Bible lessons to any size class are provided for you in the **Learning Lab**.

Challenging topics each quarter keep your kids coming back!

Group's **Hands-On Bible Curriculum** covers topics that matter to your kids and teaches them the Bible with integrity. Switching topics every month keeps your 1st- through 6th-graders enthused and coming back for more. The full two-year program will help your kids...

- •make God-pleasing decisions,
- •recognize their God-given potential, and
- •seek to grow as Christians.

Take the boredom out of Sunday school, children's church, and midweek meetings for your elementary students. Make your job easier and more rewarding with no-fail lessons that are ready in a flash. Order Group's **Hands-On Bible Curriculum** for your 1st- through 6th-graders today.

Hands-On Bible Curriculum is also available for
Toddlers & 2s, Preschool, and Pre-K and K!